Reptiles

KING COBRAS

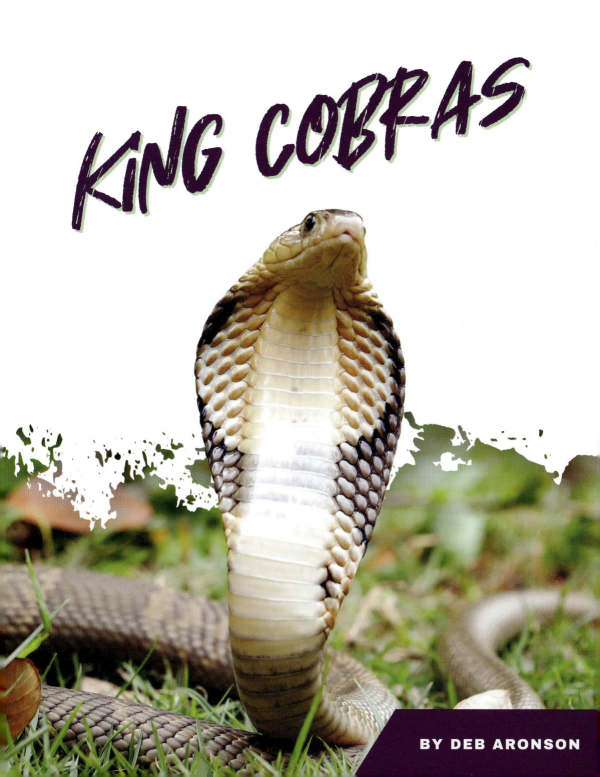

BY DEB ARONSON

WWW.APEXEDITIONS.COM

Copyright © 2024 by Apex Editions, Mendota Heights, MN 55120. All rights reserved. No part of this book may be reproduced or utilized in any form or by any means without written permission from the publisher.

Apex is distributed by North Star Editions:
sales@northstareditions.com | 888-417-0195

Produced for Apex by Red Line Editorial.

Photographs ©: Shutterstock Images, cover, 1, 4–5, 6, 7, 8, 10–11, 12–13, 14, 16–17, 18–19, 20, 28–29; iStockphoto, 21, 22–23, 26, 27; Malcolm Schuyl/ImageBROKER/FLPA/Blue Planet Archive, 24–25

Library of Congress Control Number: 2022920225

ISBN
978-1-63738-547-0 (hardcover)
978-1-63738-601-9 (paperback)
978-1-63738-706-1 (ebook pdf)
978-1-63738-655-2 (hosted ebook)

Printed in the United States of America
Mankato, MN
082023

NOTE TO PARENTS AND EDUCATORS

Apex books are designed to build literacy skills in striving readers. Exciting, high-interest content attracts and holds readers' attention. The text is carefully leveled to allow students to achieve success quickly. Additional features, such as bolded glossary words for difficult terms, help build comprehension.

TABLE OF CONTENTS

CHAPTER 1
QUICK ATTACK   4

CHAPTER 2
SNAKE LIFE   10

CHAPTER 3
HUNTING TIME   16

CHAPTER 4
LIFE CYCLE   22

COMPREHENSION QUESTIONS • 28
GLOSSARY • 30
TO LEARN MORE • 31
ABOUT THE AUTHOR • 31
INDEX • 32

CHAPTER 1

Quick Attack

A king cobra lies still on the floor of the rain forest. It flicks its forked tongue. It is looking for **prey**.

Cobras can use their tongues to pick up smells from the air.

King cobras often hide and then rush out to attack prey.

Another snake slithers by. It sees the king cobra and tries to get away. But the king cobra is faster. It strikes!

FAST FACT
A king cobra's fangs are short but very sharp.

Sometimes cobras raise their bodies before they attack.

The king cobra's fangs sink into the other snake. They pump **venom** into its body. The other snake dies, and the king cobra swallows it whole.

A DEADLY BITE

The venom in a single king cobra bite is strong enough to kill 20 people. Without treatment, a person could die just 30 minutes after being bitten.

A king cobra's fangs point backward. They help pull food into the snake's mouth.

CHAPTER 2

SNAKE LIFE

Like all snakes, king cobras are **reptiles**. King cobras can have brown, green, yellow, or black scales.

The color of a king cobra's scales often depends on where it lives.

King cobras also have **hoods**. They spread their hoods to look bigger. Cobras also raise the fronts of their bodies. They hiss and sway back and forth. This can scare other animals.

Most king cobras are between 10 and 12 feet (3 and 3.7 m) long.

FAST FACT
King cobras are the longest venomous snakes in the world. Some can grow 18 feet (5.5 m) long.

King cobras live in Asia. They usually live in rain forests. King cobras are often found near water. They also climb high in trees and bushes.

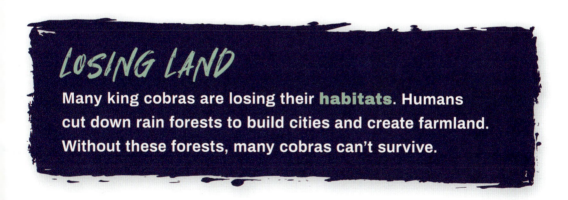

LOSING LAND

Many king cobras are losing their **habitats**. Humans cut down rain forests to build cities and create farmland. Without these forests, many cobras can't survive.

◀ King cobras spend about one-fourth of their lives up in trees.

CHAPTER 3

King cobras are **carnivores**. They mainly eat other snakes. King cobras wait quietly. Their colors help them hide. Then they strike.

King cobras can eat many kinds of snakes. They even eat other cobras.

King cobras may eat small animals such as lizards or mice.

King cobras bite prey with their sharp fangs. The fangs release venom. The venom **paralyzes** the prey.

A BIG MEAL
King cobras often eat lots of food at once. A big meal can take many days to break down. The snakes may go months before they need to eat again.

King cobras are deadly but shy. They don't often attack.

King cobras have few **predators**. The mongoose is one. Mongooses are mostly immune to king cobras' venom. It doesn't hurt them.

FAST FACT
King cobras can eat some venomous snakes. But other types can hurt them.

Mongooses are small, furry animals. They can move very quickly.

CHAPTER 4

LIFE CYCLE

King cobras usually live alone. Once a year, they come together to **mate**. Males may fight so females notice them. The males wrestle one another.

In mating season, male king cobras use their sense of smell to find females.

After mating, females build nests. They gather dead leaves into piles. Then they lay about 20 to 40 eggs.

SURPRISING SKILL

Many snakes lay eggs. But king cobras are the only snakes that build nests. King cobra females even stay on their nests to guard the eggs. The males stay close by, too.

King cobra eggs are leathery and white.

Eggs hatch a couple of months later. Then, baby king cobras leave the nest. They can live on their own right away. They can hunt, too.

Young king cobras have thin white or yellow stripes.

King cobras are fully grown after four to six years.

FAST FACT

King cobras can live up to 20 years in the wild.

COMPREHENSION QUESTIONS

Write your answers on a separate piece of paper.

1. Write a few sentences describing how a king cobra catches and eats prey.

2. King cobras mainly eat snakes. If you could eat just one type of food, what would it be?

3. What body parts help king cobras make themselves look bigger?
    - A. fangs
    - B. hoods
    - C. scales

4. Why might looking bigger help king cobras scare other animals?
    - A. Bigger animals often win fights.
    - B. Bigger animals are easier to fight.
    - C. Bigger animals move more slowly.

5. What does **immune** mean in this book?

*Mongooses are mostly **immune** to king cobras' venom. It doesn't hurt them.*

    A. killed by something
    B. not harmed by something
    C. very afraid of something

6. What does **sway** mean in this book?

*Cobras also raise the fronts of their bodies. They hiss and **sway** back and forth.*

    A. eat
    B. move
    C. swim

Answer key on page 32.

GLOSSARY

carnivores
Animals that eat meat.

habitats
The places where animals normally live.

hoods
Areas around the heads and necks of cobras.

mate
To form a pair and come together to have babies.

paralyzes
Makes something unable to move.

predators
Animals that hunt and eat other animals.

prey
Animals that are hunted and eaten by other animals.

reptiles
Cold-blooded animals that have scales.

venom
A poison made by an animal and used to bite or sting prey.

BOOKS

Downs, Kieran. *King Cobra vs. Mongoose*. Minneapolis: Bellwether Media, 2022.

Jaycox, Jaclyn. *King Cobras*. North Mankato, MN: Capstone Press, 2023.

Murray, Julie. *King Cobras*. Minneapolis: Abdo Publishing, 2020.

ONLINE RESOURCES

Visit **www.apexeditions.com** to find links and resources related to this title.

ABOUT THE AUTHOR

Deb Aronson is the author of *Alexandra the Great*, a biography of a racehorse named Rachel Alexandra. Deb loves writing about ordinary people doing extraordinary things. She lives in North Carolina with her spouse, cat, and six sailboats.

INDEX

A
Asia, 15

C
carnivores, 16

E
eggs, 24–26

F
fangs, 7, 9, 18
fight, 22

H
habitats, 15
hoods, 12

M
mating, 22, 24

N
nests, 24–26

P
predators, 20
prey, 4, 18

R
rain forests, 4, 15
reptiles, 10

T
tongue, 4

V
venom, 9, 13, 18, 20–21

ANSWER KEY:
1. Answers will vary; 2. Answers will vary; 3. B; 4. A; 5. B; 6. B